Award-Winning Sports Broadcasters

MIKE BREEN

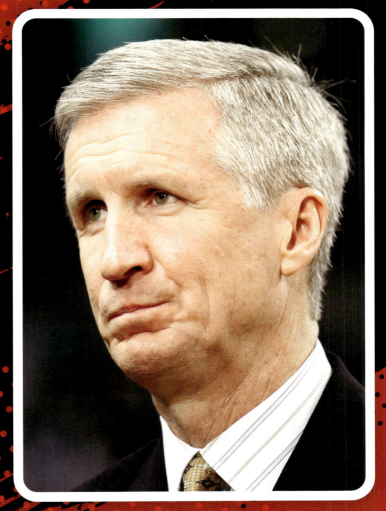

Tammy Gagne

Mitchell Lane

PUBLISHERS

2001 SW 31st Avenue
Hallandale, FL 33009
www.mitchelllanepub.com

Copyright © 2025 by Mitchell Lane Publishers. All rights reserved. No part of this book may be reproduced without written permission from the publisher. Printed and bound in the United States of America.

First Edition, 2025.
Author: Tammy Gagne
Designer: Ed Morgan
Editor: Morgan Brody

Series: Award-Winning Sports Broadcasters
Title: Mike Breen

Hallandale, FL : Mitchell Lane Publishers, [2025]

Library bound ISBN: 979-8-89260-071-2
eBook ISBN: 979-8-89260-080-4

PHOTO CREDITS: cover, p. 7, 11, 24, 27, 29, 30 Newscom.com; p. 13 Sporting News Archives, wikimedia; p. 14, 19, 20, 23, 41 wikimedia; p. 33, 38, AP Images

CONTENTS

1	**Bang!**	4
2	**Sports** and **Radio**	10
3	**Calling** the **Shots**	18
4	Making **Changes**	26
5	True **Fortune**	34

Timeline	42
Find Out More	43
Glossary	44
Works Consulted	46
Index	48
About the Author	48

CHAPTER ONE

BANG!

"**D**own by just two points, with less than a minute left on the clock, Kelsey grabs the ball back for her team! The entire championship now rests in her hands. But can she tie it up?"

"What are you talking about?" Kelsey asked Dean as she dribbled the ball toward the basketball hoop in his driveway. "We're playing a one-on-one game just for fun."

CHAPTER ONE

"Determined to turn the tide," Dean went on, "she races to the other end of the court." Kelsey chuckled while her friend spoke into his fist as if it were a microphone. As she lifted the ball and aimed, he kept up his play-by-play commentary. "Kelsey shoots. And bang! She scores!" Dean followed up his performance with sound effects. He cupped both hands around his mouth and mimicked a cheering crowd.

"What has gotten into you?" Kelsey asked as she retrieved the ball. She wasn't sure if she should pass it to him or prepare to be interviewed.

"I'm just practicing. I want to announce the high school games next year."

"Oh, you'd be perfect for that," she said. She tossed him the ball as she reached for her water bottle. "You have the voice of a sports **broadcaster**."

"Do I sound anything like Mike Breen?" he asked. They had both been watching Knicks games that Breen announced since Kelsey moved to New York two years earlier.

"Maybe a little," Kelsey replied. "But you will need to practice a lot more if you want to become a professional announcer like him." She then noticed that Dean had gotten quiet, which wasn't at all like him. "Wait, is that what you want?" she asked him.

Being a professional sports announcer comes with a lot of pressure. Even with all his experience, Mike Breen still gets nervous sometimes.

CHAPTER ONE

"I really do," her friend confessed.

"You just want to be on television," Kelsey teased. Dean did like being the center of attention. But he shook his head no.

"It's more than that," he said. "I want to be the one who gets everyone excited about what's happening on the court. A good announcer can even help turn new **spectators** into die-hard fans."

"Wouldn't you get nervous speaking in front of all those people who go to the games? Hundreds of people attend the high school games," Kelsey reminded him. "Imagine how many people listen to NBA announcers. What if you mispronounce someone's name or temporarily forget what a foul shot is called?"

"I read an interview that Mike Breen did recently," Dean shared. "He said that he still gets butterflies before big games. And he's been a professional announcer for years."

"All kidding aside, you probably know more about the game than anyone else I know," Kelsey admitted. "And you're great at getting people excited about basketball. I was a hockey fan before you introduced me to the Knicks." Then Kelsey smiled before yelling, "Bang!" She knocked the ball out of Dean's hands and started dribbling it again.

"Hey, I'm the one who gets to say that!" Dean hollered as he tried to block her next shot.

"No, you don't," Kelsey told him between breaths. "That's Mike Breen's word. If you're going to be a professional sports broadcaster, you're going to need your own catchphrase."

CHAPTER TWO

SPORTS AND RADIO

Mike Breen was born in New York City on May 22, 1961. He was the fourth child of John and Mary Breen. John had served in the U.S. Marine Corps before taking a job as a **steamfitter**. Mary stayed at home while raising their six boys. When asked about his parents during an interview with the *Athletic* website many years later, Mike called them "two of the most selfless people in the world." They raised their children to value family, community, and kindness.

CHAPTER **TWO**

Friends could spot the Breen household from a long distance. Without a clothes dryer, Mary hung the family's laundry on not just one but two long clotheslines. Mike says that some days both lines were filled with nothing but pairs and pairs of the boys' sweat socks.

Sports were a big part of life for Mike and his siblings. They played wiffle ball with neighborhood children every chance they got. As a young boy, Mike was a big baseball fan. He remembers wearing a Mets jersey every day of one summer during his childhood. He keeps a picture of himself from this era in his cell phone's photo app.

Growing up in Yonkers, Mike also became a basketball fan. His favorite Knicks players were Walt "Clyde" Frazier and Dave DeBusschere. But while other kids daydreamed about hitting homeruns or scoring three-point shots on the basketball court, Mike was taken with another pastime. He loved listening to sports announcers such as Marty Glickman and Marv Albert.

Sports and RADIO

As a young basketball fan, Mike idolized Knicks point guard Walt Frazier (left).

CHAPTER TWO

Fordham University is a private college in New York City.

Sports and RADIO

An older boy in Mike's neighborhood also had an interest in broadcasting. Tony Minecola attended the New York Institute of Technology. In his spare time, Tony built a radio station in his family's basement. Other kids often listened to Tony's shows. Mike told the *Ringer* website, "Every once in a while, instead of sitting there and listening, I'd wander in and watch what he'd do. And once he asked me, 'Would you want to do a shift?' I thought it was the coolest thing." He says this was what made him start thinking about becoming a broadcaster when he grew up.

He continued to play sports as he got older. And he was good at them. When he attended Salesian High School in New Rochelle, Mike's team even made the state semifinals. He has said he was good at shooting free throws. When it came time for college, he looked for a school with both a basketball team and a radio station. Even then, he knew that broadcasting was going to be a big part of his future. He enrolled in New York's Fordham University.

CHAPTER **TWO**

Mike got off to a bit of a rough start at his new school. Running appeared to be a regular part of the basketball team's practices. This requirement intimidated Mike, who decided not to try out for the team because of it. Although he was shy, he did want to be part of the school's radio station, WFUV. But the older students who ran it didn't make it easy for freshman. They didn't want to share their airtime with newcomers. Mike worried that he'd made a mistake going to Fordham. He was so discouraged that he almost left the school. But then he made a friend who changed everything.

SPORTS and RADIO

Mike was a good basketball player, but he knew he didn't have what it takes to play professional ball.

17

CHAPTER THREE

CALLING THE SHOTS

Michael Kay

Mike met fellow Fordham student Michael Kay at the school's radio station. The two young men began hanging out and talking about their futures. Mike told his new friend that he planned to become the announcer for the New York Knicks. In this imaginary future, Mike envisioned Kay announcing Yankees games. Other students laughed at these big dreams when they heard the friends discussing them.

CHAPTER THREE

Poughkeepsie is located in New York's Hudson River Valley region.

Calling the SHOTS

But Mike and his new friend were doing everything they could to make their career goals a reality. They spent nearly all the time they weren't in class at the station. WFUV aired a show called *One on One* that discussed sports. It was the only program like it in the area, so it picked up lots of listeners. Mike had lost enthusiasm for playing basketball himself when he entered college. But his excitement for watching others play never diminished. Each time one of the college athletes would make an especially faraway shot, now known as a three-pointer, Mike would yell, "Bang!" He quickly became known for using the word.

After graduation, Mike moved to Poughkeepsie for a job as a reporter at WEOK/WPDH. His responsibilities didn't involve sports. Instead, he covered stories about school board meetings. But he worked his way up to becoming the station's news **anchor**. Mike believed that working hard would pay off. He had also learned that it was important to try new things and push himself past his comfort zone.

CHAPTER **THREE**

Sports remained a part of his life, though. He became a certified basketball **referee**, working games in his free time. At first, he refereed fifth-grade girls' games. Later, he called men's junior college games. He is proud of the work he did while wearing the black-and-white striped shirt.

What he wanted most, though, was to announce games. After applying for a job with the Colony Sports Network, he finally got his chance. Mike covered basketball games at Poughkeepsie's Marist College alongside a more experienced announcer named Dean Darling. As the color analyst, Mike was tasked with summing up how the game was progressing when there wasn't much action happening on the court.

In an interview with Marist's online publication *Center Field*, Mike said he learned a lot from working with Darling. Mike shared, "In radio, you have to paint the picture, so you're talking all the time. You have to describe everything because the listener is unable to see the game." Darling knew when to keep going and when to take a break. And Mike paid close attention.

Calling the SHOTS

Mike finally got his shot at announcing basketball games at Marist College.

CHAPTER **THREE**

Don Imus was a controversial talk radio host in the 1990s.

Calling the SHOTS

Other people in the sports radio world began noticing Mike's broadcasting skills. In 1990, he received an offer to give sports updates on a popular WFAN radio program called *Imus in the Morning*. The work was a bit different from announcing college games. Instead of covering games live, Mike was talking about them the next day. He often joked along with the show's host, Don Imus, about professional athletes. Some listeners thought the jokes went too far while other people found the show entertaining.

Within a year, Mike received another career-changing offer. In addition to his work on *Imus in the Morning*, he began announcing Knicks games on WFAN. The goal that Mike had set for himself back in college was finally taking shape. The following year, Mike's early prediction about his best college buddy also came true. Michael Kay began announcing Yankees games on WABC Radio. The two friends had both achieved their sportscasting dreams.

CHAPTER FOUR

MAKING CHANGES

Mike Breen interviewing New York Knicks player Jamal Crawford

Mike continued working on *Imus in the Morning* by day and announcing games based on their schedule. He also made the jump from radio to television, calling NBA games on NBC. But this hectic routine took a toll on him. As his contract on the morning show neared its end, he decided to leave the program in 2000.

CHAPTER **FOUR**

"I'm tired of being tired," he told the *New York Times* when he made the announcement. "I've become a professional napper. I've been getting sick. I got **pneumonia**. And I want to spend more time with my kids." As Mike had been building his career, he married his wife, Rosanne. Together, they had three children—Michael, Nicole, and Matt.

Imus was sad to see Mike go. But he wasn't surprised that his sports guy was moving on. "His future is as a big-time sportscaster, not making fun of athletes on my program, and my advice is to pursue that," Imus said in the *New York Times* article. The big time was exactly where Mike was heading. But it almost looked like it wouldn't happen.

In 2003, NBC lost the rights to air professional basketball games. "I was pretty down because I wanted to do the NBA," Mike told the *NBA* website in a 2023 interview. Mike decided to **cold-call** Mark Shapiro, a vice president at ESPN, to ask for a job announcing NBA games for the sports network. Shapiro hired Mike on the spot, even asking him why he hadn't called sooner.

Making CHANGES

Mike with his wife, Rosanne

CHAPTER **FOUR**

Mike and Walt Frazier have made a popular announcing pair since 2004.

Making CHANGES

While Mike had been working his way up the sports radio ladder, one of his basketball idols was starting his own career in broadcasting. After ten seasons with the Knicks, Walt Frazier decided to retire from playing professional basketball. But he was far from done with the sport. Frazier began announcing games in 1987. In 2004, he started calling Knicks games with Mike. Sports fans enjoyed the chemistry between the announcing pair. Perhaps people could tell that they were also becoming good friends.

Mike also began taking on other play-by-play announcing work. In addition to the Knicks games, he also called WNBA games for NBC. He even announced NFL games for NBC and FOX. But basketball remained his top priority. He especially enjoyed doing play-by-play for the NBA Finals. And he didn't mind putting in extra time to get this job done. In 2023, Mike told *GQ* magazine, "Every series that I've ever called, I root for seven games, always." His passion for the game is still unmistakable.

CHAPTER **FOUR**

Mike had received many awards and other honors as he was making a name for himself in sports broadcasting. He was asked to announce basketball games at four consecutive Olympic Games starting in 1996. In 1998, the National Sportscasters and Sportswriters Association honored Mike as Broadcaster of the Year in New York. But one of his biggest honors came in September of 2022 when Mike won a Sports Emmy for Outstanding Personality/Play-by-Play.

Making CHANGES

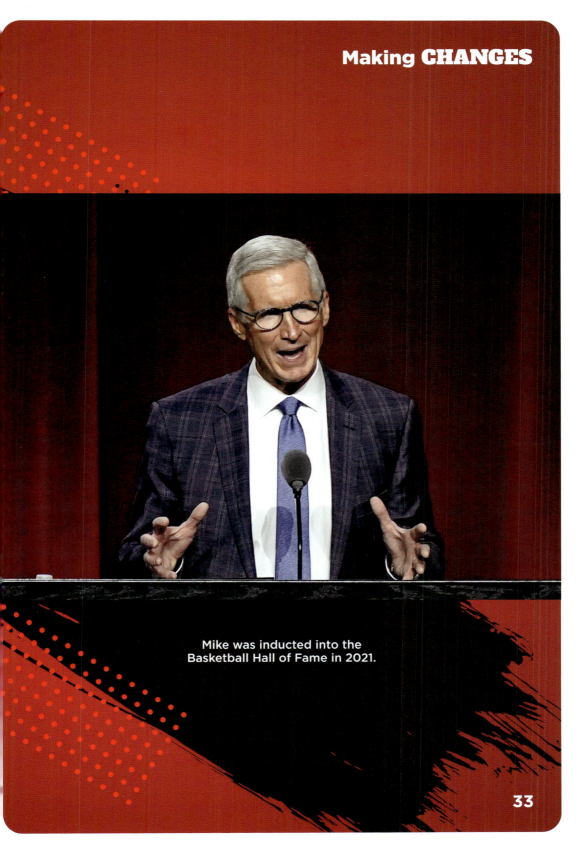

Mike was inducted into the Basketball Hall of Fame in 2021.

CHAPTER FIVE

TRUE FORTUNE

The year 2022 also brought some big challenges for Mike and his family. In October, he asked his longtime friend Michael Kay to make an announcement for him. Live on ESPN, Kay shared, "Mike and his wife Rosanne, they were in California finishing up a vacation before he starts the NBA season. They got a call right before they were getting on a plane that something had happened to [their] house. It burned to the ground. Everything was destroyed. No memories are left."

CHAPTER **FIVE**

The family was devastated. But they were also grateful. Because no one had been home at the time of the blaze, no lives were lost in this unexpected event. Even before Kay's announcement, news of the fire was making its way through Mike's friends, **colleagues**, and fans. Many of these people phoned Mike, wanting to offer their support. Too many calls were coming in for Mike to answer. He was busy reaching out to insurance agents and trying to find clothes to wear until he could replace some of what the family had lost in the fire. Kay was there to reassure everyone that Mike was okay. He added that Mike "considers himself absolutely blessed for the people that have reached out and asked to help."

Mike's brothers were among the many people who made phone calls that day. When they first heard about the fire, they didn't know that Mike and Rosanne weren't home. Mike said he will never forget the way their voices sounded as they left messages, asking him to let them know he and his family were alright.

True FORTUNE

The fire at Mike and Rosanne's home left the property a total loss. They weren't able to salvage any of their possessions.

CHAPTER **FIVE**

Many other people would have taken some time off after losing their house in a fire. But Mike wanted to move on with his life without delay.

True FORTUNE

    Mike is especially thankful that his younger son, Matt, wasn't home at the time the fire broke out. Before his trip, Mike asked his son to take the family's golden retriever to their beach house. Mike had arranged to have the floors redone while they were away, and he didn't want the dog to walk on them before they were ready. Matt, however, just wanted to stay home. He assured his father that he would keep the dog off the floors. At the last minute, Matt agreed to go to the beach house instead. Mike believes this decision saved his youngest child's life.

    Eventually, life returned to normal following the loss of the Breen home. Mike refused to delay his return to work. He also refused to feel sorry for himself, despite losing nearly everything he ever owned. He pointed out that he was fortunate to have insurance. He realized that many people who had experienced a fire didn't have that luxury. His parents had taught him to focus on the truly important things in life. For him, that was his family. He also still felt fortunate to do something he enjoyed so much for a living.

CHAPTER **FIVE**

In 2023, Mike reached a milestone in his career. He called his 100th NBA Finals broadcast. Only two other NBA announcers had called more finals games. LA Lakers announcer Chick Hearn had called the most at 121. Next, there was Boston Celtics announcer Johnny Most with 103. Mike almost didn't even realize what was happening. Someone else had to tell him it was his 100th finals game. He told the *NBA* website, "For some reason, to hear that number was surprising to me, and it's not something even in my wildest dreams that I thought I could do."

True FORTUNE

Mike feels fortunate that he has had his dream job for more than three decades.

TIMELINE

1961 Mike Breen is born in New York City on May 22.

1979 He graduates from Salesian High School in New Rochelle, New York.

1983 Mike graduates from Fordham University.

He starts working at WEOK/WPDH in Poughkeepsie.

1990 He begins giving sports updates on the radio program *Imus in the Morning*.

1991 Mike begins announcing Knicks games on WFAN.

1996 He is asked to announce basketball at the first of four Olympic Games.

1997 Mike moves from radio to television announcing, calling NBA games on NBC.

1998 He is named Broadcaster of the Year by the National Sportscasters and Sportswriters Association.

2000 He decides to leave *Imus in the Morning* to focus on his play-by-play work.

2003 Mike lands a new job, announcing basketball on ESPN.

2004 He starts working alongside his longtime idol Walt Frazier.

2022 Mike receives a Sports Emmy for Outstanding Personality/Play-by-Play.

A fire burns Mike's home to the ground.

2023 He calls his 100th NBA Finals, becoming just the third person to reach this milestone.

FIND OUT MORE

PRINT

Davidson, B. Keith. *WNBA*, New York, NY: Crabtree Publishing Company, 2022.

Gagne, Tammy. *Malika Andrews*. Hallandale, FL: Mitchell Lane Publishers, 2024.

Kjartansson, Kjartan Atli. *Legends of the NBA*. New York, NY: Abbeville Kids, 2022.

ON THE INTERNET

Andres, Patrick. "Celebrate Mike Breen's 100th NBA Finals Games with His Best 'Bang!' Calls," *Sports Illustrated*, June 12, 2023.
www.si.com/nba/2023/06/12/celebrate-mike-breen-milestone-with-bang-call-compilation

ESPN
https://www.espn.com

NBA
www.nba.com

GLOSSARY

anchor
A newscaster whose primary job is reporting the news

broadcaster
A person who delivers the news on television

cold-call
To call a person without prior contact

colleagues
The people with whom a person works

pneumonia
An illness involving the lungs

referee
A sports official with final authority regarding a game

steamfitter
A person who installs or repairs pipes, such as those for heating

spectators
People who attend an event such as a game to watch it

WORKS CONSULTED

Baker, Katie. "A Voice from Radio," *The Ringer*, June 8, 2016. https://www.theringer.com/2016/6/8/16037814/mike-breen-2016-nba-finals-new-york-knicks-tv-voice-5ec2f8f2a1co.

Beck, Howard. "Bang! Mike Breen on 18 Years of Calling the NBA Finals," *GQ*, June 6, 2023. https://www.gq.com/story/mike-breen-interview-nba-finals-2023.

DiGiovani, Sam. "McCann to MSG: A One-on-One with Mike Breen on How Covering Marist Men's Basketball Shaped His Career," *Center Field*, February 16, 2022. https://centerfieldmarist.com/2022/02/16/mccann-to-msg-a-one-on-one-with-mike-breen-on-how-covering-marist-mens-basketball-shaped-his-career.

"History of the 3-Pointer," *USA Basketball*, January 1, 2014. https://www.usab.com/news/2014/01/history-of-the-3-pointer.

"Mike Breen," Wasserman, n.d. https://www.teamwass.com/speaker/mike-breen/#:~:text=A%20Fordham%20University%20graduate%2C%20Breen,WPDH%20in%20Poughkeepsie%2C%20New%20York.

Reedy, Joe. "ESPN's Mike Breen Calls His 100th NBA Finals Broadcast in Game 5," *NBA*, June 12, 2023. https://www.nba.com/news/espn-mike-breen-100th-nba-finals-broadcast-game-5.

Reidy, Darren. "NBA Commentator Mike Breen: The Man in the Middle," *Men's Journal*, December 4, 2017. https://www.mensjournal.com/sports/nba-commentator-mike-breen-the-man-in-the-middle-w209963.

Sandomir, Richard. "Plus: Radio; Breen to Leave the Imus Show," *The New York Times*, January 8, 2000. https://www.nytimes.com/2000/01/08/sports/plus-radio-breen-to-leave-the-imus-show.html.

Thompson, Marcus II. "Thompson: Love and Support Got Mike Breen Voice of NBA Finals, Through the Fire," *The Athletic*, June 1, 2023. https://theathletic.com/4564752/2023/06/01/mike-breen-fire-home-recovery.

"Walt 'Clyde' Frazier," *MSG Network*, n.d. https://www.msgnetworks.com/personalities/walt-clyde-frazier/#:~:text=The%20former%20Knicks%20star%20began,in%20his%20hometown%20of%20Atlanta.

"Walt Frazier Earns Second Basketball Hall of Fame Nod, This Time as a Broadcaster," *The Athletic*, February 18, 2022. https://theathletic.com/4182160/2022/02/18/walt-frazier-earns-second-basketball-hall-of-fame-nod-this-time-as-broadcaster.

INDEX

Albert, Marv, 12
Breen, John, 11, 39
Breen, Mary, 11, 39
Breen, Matt, 28, 39
Breen, Michael (son), 28
Breen, Mike
  awards, 32
  birth, 11
  catchphrase, 9, 21
  childhood, 11–15
  education, 15–16, 19–21
  refereeing, 22
Breen, Nicole, 28
Breen, Rosanne, 28, 35, 36
Darling, Dean, 22
DeBusschere, Dave, 12
ESPN, 28, 35
fire, 35–36, 39

Fordham University, 15, 16, 19
Frazier, Walt, 12, 31
Glickman, Marty, 12
Hearn, Chick, 40
Imus, Don, 25, 28
Imus in the Morning, 25, 27
Kay, Michael, 19, 25, 35, 36
Most, Johnny, 40
NBA, 8, 27, 28, 31, 35, 40
NBC, 27, 28, 31
New York Knicks, 6, 9, 12, 19, 25, 31
Salesian High School, 15
WEOK/WPDH, 21
WFAN, 25
WFUV, 16, 21
WNBA, 31

ABOUT THE AUTHOR

Tammy Gagne is a freelance writer and editor who specializes in educational nonfiction for young people. She has written hundreds of books on a wide range of topics. Some of her favorite projects have been about journalists and athletes. Tammy's other books in the **Award-Winning Broadcasters** series include *Malika Andrews* and *Mike Tirico*.